ART NOUVEAU

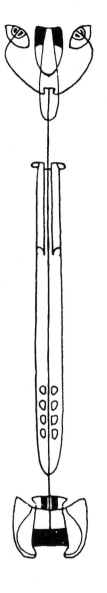

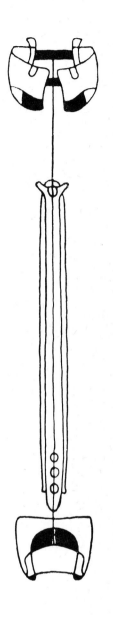

ART NOUVEAU
Graphics

edited by

Thomas Walters

ACADEMY EDITIONS LONDON

st. martin's press   new york

We should like to thank the Victoria and Albert Museum for permission to reproduce illustrations; Marlborough Graphics for providing material from their Exhibition of Secessionist painters; Mr. Godfrey Pilkington of the Piccadilly Gallery and Mr. Victor Arwas of Editions Graphiques for their advice and help in supplying photographs.

First published in Great Britain in 1971 by Academy Editions, Holland Street, London W8.
Revised edition 1972. Reprinted 1972.
© 1971,1972 by Academy Editions. All rights reserved.
Designed by Prantong Jitasiri.

First published in the United States of America in 1972 by
St. Martin's Press, 175 Fifth Avenue, New York, N.Y. 10010.
Library of Congress Catalog Card Number 78 - 185851.

Reproduced and printed by photolithography, and bound in Great Britain
at The Pitman Press, Bath

INTRODUCTION

Art Nouveau is a term that can be used to classify any one of a dozen styles in Western applied and fine art - each one apparently unique and self-contained, yet all part of a movement that was linked to a determination to shock, to revolt, and above all, to change. The growing homogeneity of Western civilization is evidenced by the speed at which Art Nouveau grew, for the movement hardly lasted thirty years - from about 1885 until the first world war - and it was past its peak of inventivness half way through that time.

Throughout Europe a host of different names bore witness to the new style. Thus in France it was known as *Style Moderne,* or *Style Nouille* (because of the noodle-like tresses of hair that adorned the girls in most Art Nouveau posters). In Germany, it was known as *Jugendstil,* in Austria as *Sezessionstil* and in Spain as *Modernista.* The term Art Nouveau itself was invented only in 1895 when Samuel Bing opened his shop "La Maison de l'Art Nouveau" in Paris.

Art Nouveau - if these things can be said to start in any one place - started in England. England was the natural breeding ground for such an artistic revolt, for in the second half of the nineteenth century William Morris and his Arts and Crafts movement, the Pre-Raphaelites, and the Aesthetic movement, for all their failings reacted not only against tawdry neo-classicism and academic traditionalism but tried to bring art to terms with the machine age. It is through these revolutionary art movements that the long sinuous line - like a whiplash - that is the hallmark of Art Nouveau was inherited from William Blake.

The emergence and continued existence of the new style, which, with all its trappings of sly and dandified decadence was as much opposed to the Arts and Crafts movement and the Pre-Raphaelites as these movements were to those that had preceeded them, is above all the product of two men. Arthur Heygate Mackmurdo, and Aubrey Vincent Beardsley. Both Mackmurdo and Beardsley started their otherwise totally different artistic careers as followers of Morris and the Pre-Raphaelites.

Mackmurdo later on set up an architectural practice and started the Hobby-Horse (page 21). This magazine was the journal of the Century Guild - the first group to revolt from Morris whose once-revolutionary return to gothic was stultifying into conservative historicism. One of Mackmurdo's earliest design was for a book cover for 'Wren's City Churches' (page 23). In ten years time this would be the model for a completely new style. A style that was to become introverted and narcissistic without ever quite loosing the essential qualities of Mackmurdo's design.

Beardsley's life seems rather like a reflection of the life of the whole Art Nouveau movement. He lived for only twenty-eight years and drew only during the last six or seven of those, after being encouraged by Burne-Jones. Beardsley succeeded in establishing a completely new style in which the decorative value of line dividing plane surfaces replaced the three dimensional representation of reality; an emphasis which was fundemental to the development of Art Nouveau and from Beardsley is adopted by artists as diverse as Bradley and Klimt.

The influence on Art Nouveau which makes it more than just part of the ever-changing and evolving art scene is the effect of the introduction of Japanese art to Europe. In the middle eighteen-fifties trade with Japan began, and in exchange for European investment in the Far East, Japanese prints, woodcuts and objects of all sorts flowed into Paris and London. The value of Japanese art was that in presenting an entirely different graphic tradition, it gave artists a new starting point for the development of a style no longer based solely on their European artistic inheritance. The flat, nervous faces in Toulouse-Lautrec's posters, the perspectiveless mosaics of Beardsley and the linear development of drapery on Mucha's women are all witnesses to this new catalyst.

The extraordinary vitality of Art Nouveau, while it lasted, can be seen by the immediate way in which it grew from its British and Japanese origins and became the national style of so many different countries.

The Art Nouveau of France was distinguished, in that it was only in that country that it took on a primarily applied form. Underground stations, furniture, and above all bibelots, jewellery and glass became infused with the new writhing and twisting plastic plant forms; the work of Galle and Guimard became famous throughout the world, and also the newly built avenues and boulevards of Paris had their emptiness filled up by a wealth of multi-coloured posters.

In Vienna, the only apparent connection between Sezessionstil and Western Art Nouveau was the sense of violent revolt that accompanied the two. This was even stronger in Vienna than in England because the Austrian revolt lacked the cushioning effect of the Pre-Raphaelites and the Arts and Crafts movement. The Vienna Secession building which was built in 1898 has engraved above the main doorway the words "To each time its own art: to that art its freedom". This was the slogan of revolution in a city where almost every single public building aped the renaissance in the most superficial way possible.

In the German Empire too, the reaction against the lack of artistic sensibility not only of the Prussian aristocracy but of the new middle class had started. *Jugendstil* began in Munich with the tapestries of Herman Obrist and soon took on a form not unlike floral English Art Nouveau. Its leading artist was Otto Eckmann (pages 59, 63) after whose death a new and abstract, almost architectural, style grew up.

The impact of Austro-German Art Nouveau was caused in part by its seriousness: for where the French produced hundreds of gay, and colourful posters and thousands of objects d'art and bibelots, the Secessionists especially were determined to carefully build up a whole revolutionary way of life in which literally every object with which man is in contact in his daily life - whether a lavatory seat of an underground station, was designed to meet the ideals of the Secession. In no other parts of the world did the apostles of the new art achieve anything like the savagery and violence of Schiele or the high principles of the Secession. Tinged with decedence in England, frivolous in France, in Austria Art Nouveau's revolutionary emphasis can best be appreciated.

To say that Art Nouveau was killed off by the first world war, as so many of its artists were, is basically true, in that the style certainly did not survive it - but the war and Art Nouveau were products of very much the same social forces. Since the defeat of Napoleon, growing industrialization was changing the basis of European society; the spread of nationalism, socialism and communism challenged the accepted structures of political power. Yet apart from occasional tremors and upheavals such as the events of 1848, the outward forms of law, bureaucracy and government in Europe remained basically unchanged - ossified in the conservative reaction that followed Waterloo. Just as the first world war was the final deadly political symptom of this dochotomy - a bloodletting that finally rid Europe of the old empires, so was Art Nouveau an earlier intellectual symptom.

But where Art Nouveau was unique amongst all the art movements was in its combination of the old and new. Art Nouveau represented a combination of the innocent strength of the new forces together with the experienced but dying taste of the old. It was the only non-violent release of tension that could be allowed in European society. This was to some extent recognised. Mucha's posters were considered by many to be part of a plot to corrupt the young. The Austrian Emperor, Franz Joseph was so outraged by Secessionist architecture that he forbade his coachmen ever to drive past Adolf Loos' buildings. The public indignation at the time of the Wilde trials was such that *The Yellow Book* offices were stoned and one reviewer referring to Beardsley's drawings, publicly expressed the view that 'this sort of thing' should be suppressed by act of Parliament. So although Art Nouveau had an irreproachable artistic pedigree, it must be seen for what it was - the last sign of life in a dying society.

Andrew Melvin, 1971.

The Plates

AB

49.	Eugene Grasset	Encre Marquet Poster
50.	Felicien Rops	La Fleur Lascive
51.	Eugene Grasset	The Drug Addict
52.	Helen Hay	Almanac
53.	Alphonse Mucha	Moet & Chandon and Nectar
54.	Georges de Feure	Les Jardines d'Armide
55.	Georges de Feure	La Charmeuse d'Oiseux
56.	Alphonse Mucha	Topaz from The Four Precious Stones
57.	Privat-Livemont	Bitter Oriental
58.	Angelo Jank	Jugend Cover
59.	Otto Eckmann	Jugend Cover
60.	Friedrich Konig	Ver Sacrum Calender
61.	Carl Moll	Hohe Wart
62.	Koloman Moser	Book-plate
63.	Otto Eckmann	The Crab
64.	Theodore Heine	Simplicissimus Cover
65.	Franz Wacik	Midnight Feast
66.	Van Rysselberghe	Almanack Illustration
67.	Van Averbeke	Calender Illustration
68.	Anonymous	Vignettes
69.	Alberto Baruffi	Illustrations
70.	Leon Solon	The Birth of Aphrodite
71.	Paul Berthon	Portrait of Sarah Bernhardt
72.	Felix Volloton	Les Girls
73.	Gerda Wegener	Illustration
74.	Will Bradley	The Inland Printer Cover
75.	Will Bradley	Victor Bicycles Poster
76.	Will Bradley	Bradley: His Book
	Will Bradley	The Inland Printer Cover
	Will Bradley	The Inland Printer Cover
77.	Will Bradley	Victor Bicycles Poster
78.	John Sloane	Poster for Moods
	John Sloane	Two designs
79.	Louis Rhead	Poster for The Sun
80.	Louis Rhead	Exhibition Poster
81.	Louis Rhead	Lundborg's Perfumes Poster
82.	Scotson Clarke	New York Recorder Poster
83.	E. B. Bird	Mechanic's Fair Poster
	E. B. Bird	Cover for The Red Letter
84.	E. Reed	Design for Poster
	O. Giannini	Turner Brassworks Poster
85.	J. J. Gould	Lippincott's Magazine Cover
	J. J. Gould	Lippincott's Magazine Cover

WILLIAM HOLMAN HUNT. **Illustration to the Lady of Shalott,** 1857

This very interesting early drawing by Hunt, upon which his later oil painting was based, illustrates the first employment of themes, especially the decorative treatment of hair, that were to become conventions in both Art Nouveau and Symbolist Art towards the end of the century.

12

WILLIAM MORRIS and EDWARD BURNE-JONES. **Trial page for Sigurd the Volsung**, 1897. (Victoria & Albert Museum). The combination of Morris' borders and Burne-Jones' illustrations in this trial page printed by the Kelmscott Press, brings together two of the most important influences on the development of Art Nouveau in England and subsequently on the Continent.

FREDERICK WALKER. **Poster for A Woman in White by Wilkie Collins,** 1871
WALTER CRANE. **Illustration to Flora's Feast.**
Both Walker's poster and Crane's drawing show two early sources for conventions adopted by many Art Nouveau artists. Walker's design was one of the first to use black as an integral decorative feature of the poster. Crane, whose commercial designs and illustrative work were as greatly admired on the Continent as in England, developed an emphasis on flowing line.

The little Lilies of the Vale,
White ladies delicate & pale;

15

More than any other artist, Aubrey Beardsley personifies Art Nouveau. His individual style, subordinating Pre-Raphaelite and Japanese influences to a completely personal deployment of line, was the source and inspiration of countless contemporary artists who adopted decorative conventions established by him but rarely achieved his originality and elegance.

Border design from Le Morte d'Arthur, 1893.

WRENS CITY CHURCHES

BY
A·H·MACKMURDO, A·R·I·B·A,
1883
G.ALLEN, SUNNYSIDE, ORPINGTON, KENT.

W. OSPOVAT. **Bookplate,** 1896.

SELWYN IMAGE. **Cover for The Tragic Mary,** n.d.
Image worked closely with Mackmurdo and together
with him founded The Century Guild.

R. ANNING BELL. **Bookplate,** 1898.

ARTHUR MACKMURDO. Cover for The Century Guild Hobby Horse, 1884.

23

AUBREY BEARDSLEY. Cover for The Yellow Book, 1894
At twenty-three, Beardsley was appointed art editor of *The Yellow Book*.

AUBREY BEARDSLEY. Illustration from **Le Morte d'Arthur**, 1893-4.
Le Morte d'Arthur was Beardsley's first major commission.

AUBREY BEARDSLEY. **Third Tableau from Das Rhiengold, 1896.**

AUBREY BEARDSLEY.   The Cave of Spleen from The Rape of The Lock, 1897

CHARLES RICKETTS. **Title page for Nimphidia and the Muses Elizium.** Vale Press, 1896.

The Vale Press was founded in 1896 by Ricketts who designed many of its fonts, initials and borders. He was a prolific and influential painter, sculptor and writer whose work owes much to Morris, Beardsley and Japanese graphic tradition.

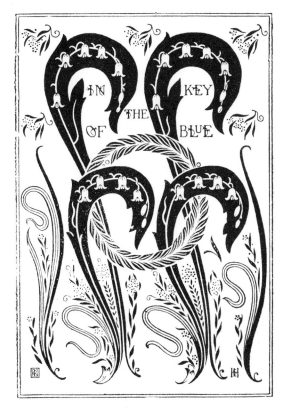

CHARLES RICKETTS. **The Moon-Horned Io,** 1894. Illustration for The Sphinx by Oscar Wilde.
Two book covers. 1891 and 1892.

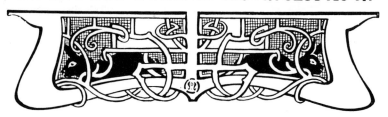

CHRISTOPHER DEAN. **Design for Book Cover,** 1898.
STUDIO COMPETITION. **Book Covers,** 1897.
Book binding, covers, title pages and plates are amongst the most attractive
examples of Art Nouveau design and graphics. They received attention and
discussion unparelled before and after the period.

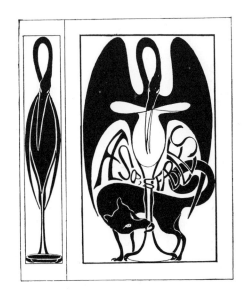

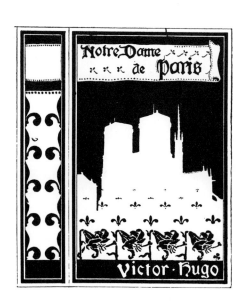

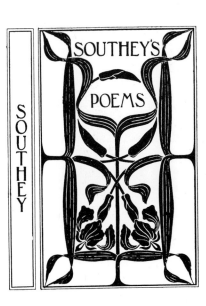

JESSIE M. KING.   1872-1948.
The Little Princess and the Peacock.
Illustration, 1902.
The Magic Grammar.
Illustration, 1902.
Trained at South Kensington and sub-
sequently at the Glasgow School of
Art, Jessie M. King became a leading
illustrator of fairy stories and child-
ren's books in the northern, 'Celtic'
Art Nouveau tradition.   Her light
delicate style and decorative fantasy
set a frequently emulated fashion.

32

WILL BRADLEY. **Cover Design**, 1895.

WILL BRADLEY. **Cover for The Chap Book.**
The Chap Book, an art magazine founded in Chicago in 1892,
became a platform for Art Nouveau in the States, comparable to *Die
Jugend* in Germany or *The Studio* in England.

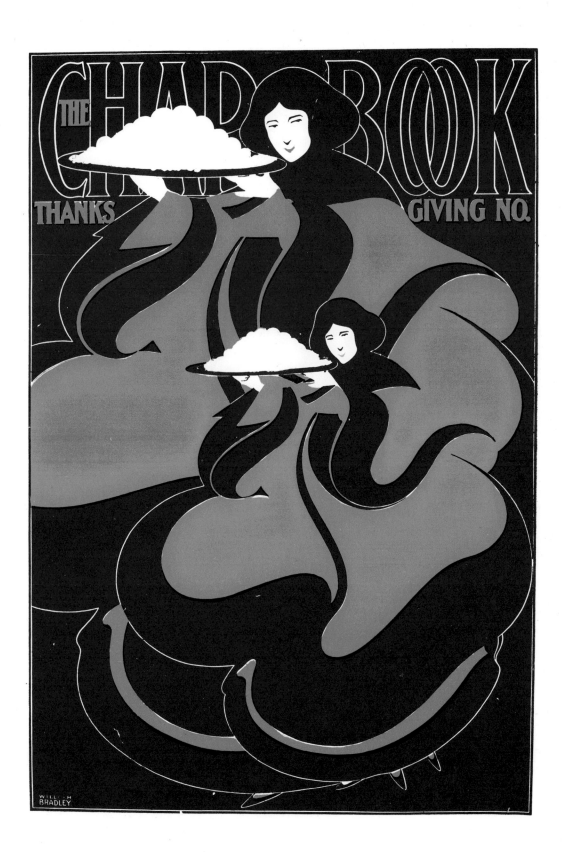

ALASTAIR. (Hans Voigt). **Lulu**, 1913. Illustration from *Erdgeist* by Wedekind. (Georg Muller Verlag, Munich).

ALASTAIR. (Hans Voigt). **"Ah, je t'aime Escamille."** 1914. Illustration from *Forty Three Drawings with a Note of Eclamation by Robert Ross*. (John Lane, The Bodley Head Ltd.)

Alastair, the pseudonym of a German who spent much of his life in England and the States, was a follower of Beardsley. His delicate, often equivocal drawings, were largely published in limited editions.

LAURENCE HOUSMAN. Illustration from
The End of Elfintown, 1904.

LAURENCE HOUSMAN. Illustration from
A Farm in Fairyland, 1904.
Housman, a talented illustrator, was a disciple
of Ricketts but developed a powerful Pre-
Raphaelite style of his own.

W.B. MACDOUGALL. Illustration from Songs of Love and Death, 1898.

ELLEN E. HOUGHTON. **Poster,** 1899. R. ANNING BELL, **Poster,** n.d.
ANONYMOUS. **Design for Book Cover** c. 1897. (Victoria & Albert Museum).

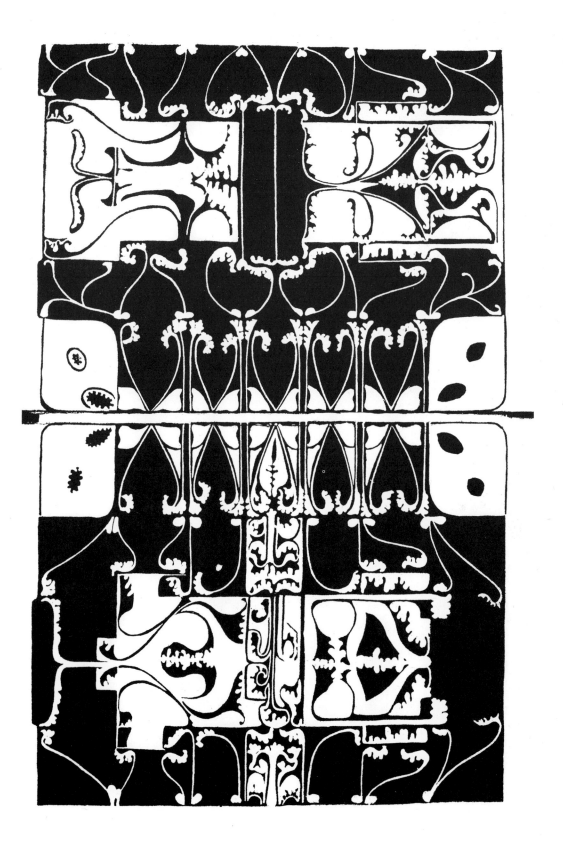

41

OLIVE ALLEN. **Illustration for a Poem.** 1901 (The Studio)

ANNIE FRENCH. **The Daisy Chain.** Illustration, 1906

42

ANNIE FRENCH. **The Picture Book.** Illustration, 1906

Thinking of little Alice

CHARLES ROBINSON.   Illustration from Alice in Wonderland.   Cassell & Co., 1908.

WILLIAM HORTON. **The Way of a Soul,** 1910. From William Thomas Horton, a study of his work, Ingpen Grant, 1919.

EUGENE GRASSET. L'Etude, n.d.

EUGENE GRASSET. **Cover for Six Contes by Jules Lemaitre,** 1894.
Grasset's lyrical grace of line and romantic mediaevalism makes him one of the most attractive and individual Art Nouveau artists. His influence was greater on the Continent and in the States than in England, giving rise to a school in which the new graphic traditions were allied to a conscious historicism.

46

EUGENE GRASSET. Design for The Grafton Gallery poster, 1893.

Verneuil.   **Poster for Dentifrices du Docteur Pierre**, n.d.
Verneuil was a prolific and talented disciple of Grasset.

EUGENE GRASSET. **Encre Marquet.** Poster, 1829. (The Victoria & Albert Museum).

FELICIEN ROPS. Title page for **La Fleur Lascive**, n.d. (Victor Arwas)

EUGENE GRASSET. **The Drug Addict**, 1898 (Piccadilly Gallery, London)

HELEN HAY. **Almanac.** From *The Evergreen*, Part III, 1896.

ALPHONSE MUCHA. **Posters for Moete Chandon and Nectar.** 1899 (Jiri Mucha)
Mucha's individual and subtle colouring which enhanced but never dominated his essentially linear compositions is well illustrated in these posters.

GEORGES DE FEURE. **Les Jardines d'Armide,** c 1896
La Charmeuse d'Oiseux, c 1897

De Feure's first ambition was to be a writer but having little success
he turned to art in 1900. A talented lithographer, illustrator, poster
designer and painter, many of his works were inspired by the leading
French Symbolist writers. His most famous work was the series
Feminiflores, in which the women and flowers which had always
dominated his subject matter became one.

ALPHONSE MUCHA. **Topaz, from The Four Precious Stones,** 1900. (Jiri Mucha). Mucha became established as the leading decorative artist in France with a poster, *Gismonda,* that he designed for Sarah Bernhardt in 1894. A master of elegant line and intricate composition, the influence of his style was such that, for a time, Art Nouveau was known as *Le Style Mucha* in France.

PRIVAT-LIVEMONT. **Bitter Oriental.** Poster, 1895. (Victoria and Albert Museum).
A successful and prolific poster designer, Privat-Livemont's style owed much to Mucha.

ANGELO JANK. **Cover for Jugend**, 1899. (Victoria & Albert Museum).
In 1896 Georg Horth, a member of the Vienna Secession, founded the Munich
magazine, *Die Jugend* which became a platform for the dissemination of Art
Nouveau, giving its name, *Jugendstil*, to the German movement.

OTTO ECKMANN. **Cover for Jugend.** (Victoria & Albert Museum).

SONDERHEFT

VER SACRUM
KALENDER
1903

FRIEDRICH KONIG. Cover for Ver Sacram Calender, 1903
(Marlborough Graphics Ltd).

CARL MOLL. **Hohe Wart.** Woodcut n.d. (Marlborough Graphics Ltd.)
Moll was a founder member of the Secession.

KOLOMAN MOSER. **Book Plate**, n.d. (Stuart Durant)

Moser, a designer, worked closely with Hoffmann and Olbrich on the exhibition hall for the Vienna Secession. He was associated with the leading Secession magazine *Ver Sacrum* for which he did many of the page ornaments.

OTTO ECKMAN. **The Crab**, illustration in Jugend, 1899. (The Piccadilly Gallery, London)

THOMAS THEODOR HEINE.   **Cover for Simplicissimus.**
Heine, a frequent contributor to *Jugend* as well as the
satirical magazine *Simplicissimus,* developed his own dis-
tinctive graphic style blending Art Nouveau elegance with a
Germanic black humour.

FRANZ WACIK. **The Midnight Feast**, 1911. (Marlborough Graphics Ltd.)

VAN RYSSELBERGHE. **Illustration from Almanack,** 1899. Dietrich et Cie.
Van Rysselberghe designed the famous first issue of *Le Libre Esthetique*, which acted as a focus
for new developments in art in Belgium.

E. VAN AVERBEKE. **Drawing for a Calender**, 1900
Van Averbeke was a member of the avant-garde de Skeldon club of Antwerp.

Vignettes for ending a story. Competition page in The Studio, 1900

ALBERTO BARUFFI. **Illustrations**, 1902.

Self-taught, Baruffi was one of the few Italian artists who whole heartedly accepted English Art Nouveau graphic conventions, reacting against the classic tradition within which the majority of his contemporaries still worked.

LEON SOLON. **The Birth of Aphrodite.**
Illustration, c. 1899.
A successful *salon* exhibitor, Solon's style reflect-
ed whatever trends in art were fashionable at the time.

PAUL BERTHON. **Portrait of Sarah Bernhardt.** n.d. (Editions Graphiques)

Berthon, whose style was greatly influenced by Grasset, produced a series of very attractive
posters but was chiefly known as a designer of murals.

GERDA WEGENER. **Illustration.** c.1904

FELIX VOLLOTON. **Les Girls.** 1902 (Editions Graphiques)

73

WILL BRADLEY. **Cover for the Inland Printer,** 1895
WILL BRADLEY. **Poster for Victor Bicycles,** n.d.

WILL BRADLEY. Cover for The Inland
Printer, 1894.

WILL BRADLEY. Prospectus for Bradley:
His Book, 1896.
Bradley His Book was an art journal, concen-
trating on new developments in graphic and
typographical design. It was not successful
and few issues were published.

WILL BRADLEY. Cover for The Inland
Printer, 1894. This was the first magazine
to change its covers monthly.

WILL BRADLEY. Section of a poster for Victor Bicycles. c. 1899
This poster was later adapted for Bar-lock typewriters.

JOHN SLOANE.   Poster for Moods, 1895
JOHN SLOANE.   Two Designs, c. 1896

LOUIS RHEAD. Design for a Poster for The Sun, 1906.

LOUIS RHEAD. **Poster for Exhibition**, c. 1893
LOUIS RHEAD. **Poster for Lundborg's Perfumes**, n.d.
The influence of Grasset, a personal friend, is apparent
in all Rhead's work.

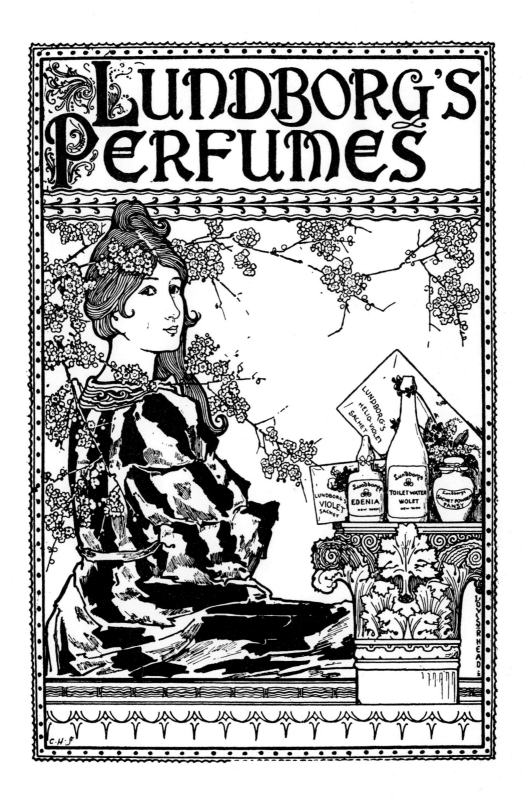

SCOTSON CLARK. **Poster for The New York Recorder, 1895.**
Scotson Clark, editor of the successful *Century* Magazine was a
schoolfellow of Beardsley and did much to popularize the new
school of poster designing in the States.

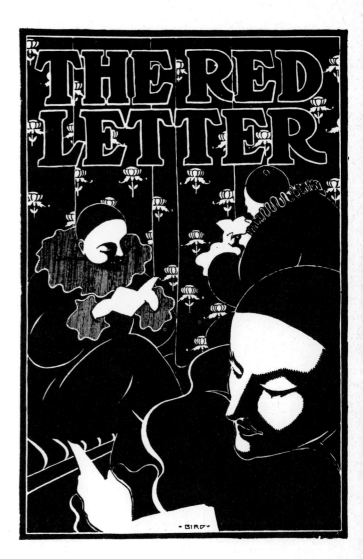

E. B. BIRD **Poster for the Mechanics Fair,** 1895   E. B. BIRD. **Cover for The Red Letter,** 1894

Bird, a colleague of Bradley was one of the most popular poster artists at the height of the collecting craze in the 'nineties. His work, though talented, was largely derivitive and tended to reflect the obvious graphic fashions of the moment.

O. GIANNINI. **Poster for The Turner Brassworks,**
1895. This remarkable design by an otherwise
little known artist has few contemporary parallels.

E. REED. **Design for Poster.** c. 1895

84

J. J. GOULD. JR. **Covers for Lippincott's Magazine**, 1896.

Gould designed several covers for this successful literary monthly. Without any starting originality, his work is consistently elegant and graceful.

Index of Artists